Wheels

C O N T E N T S

Wheels

Rolling along

Most vehicles that travel along the ground have wheels — from the smallest skateboard to the biggest truck. Their wheels help them to move.

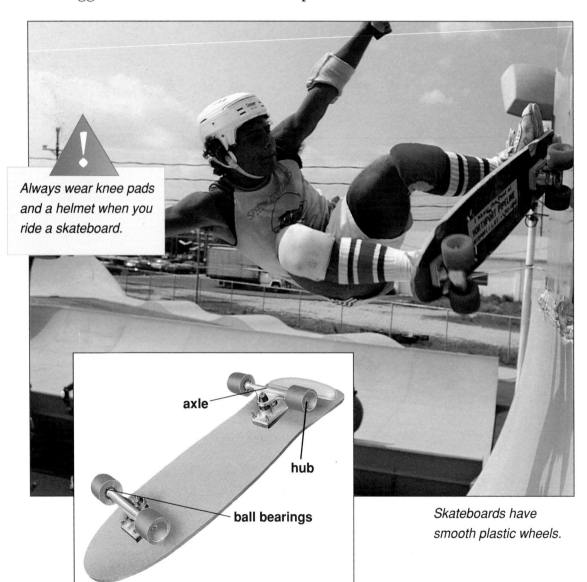

Always wear knee pads and a helmet when you ride a skateboard.

axle

hub

ball bearings

Skateboards have smooth plastic wheels.

Trucks are so heavy that they have extra wheels to help carry the load.

All wheels move by rolling.

They don't rub. They don't drag.

They roll quickly and easily along the ground.

Carrying a load

Wheels make things easy to move. Dragging a heavy sack is hard work. The sack rubs against the ground. It catches on all the bumps.

Take care! You can hurt yourself by pulling a heavy load.

Using a wheelbarrow solves the problem.
The wheel doesn't rub, it turns.
It makes the sack much easier to move.

Wheels are fitted to a lot of heavy things.
They save people having to carry . . .

suitcases . . .

furniture . . .

the shopping . . .

or young children.

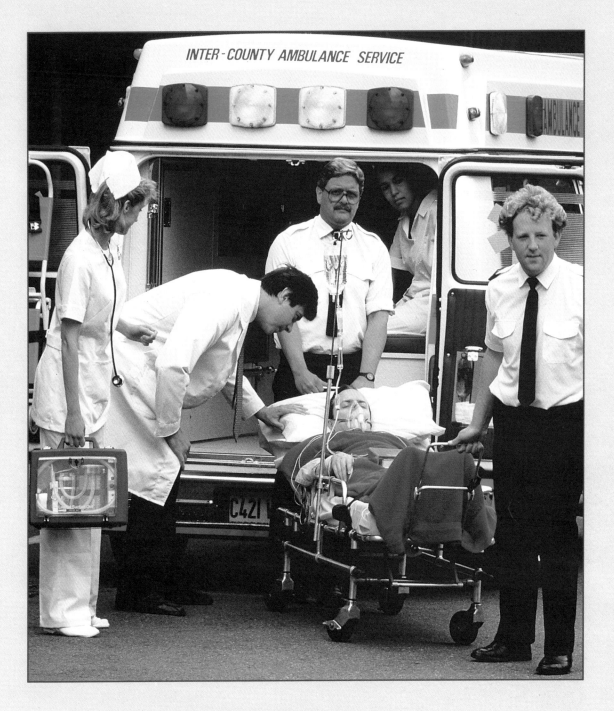

Wheels are a great help in hospitals.

Carrying a person is heavy work.

Wheeling a trolley is not.

Wheels and power

Wheels don't move by themselves.
They need power to turn them.
Sometimes the power comes from an engine.
Sometimes it comes from a horse.

Wheelchair

Car

Tricycle

Train

Bus

Sometimes people push the wheels along. They push them with their hands, or turn pedals with their feet.

Rickshaw

Racing car

Bicycle

Horse and cart

Tyres

Riding on air

Most wheels have tyres on them. Each tyre is pumped up with air. The air helps the wheels to roll over bumps in the road. It makes the ride much more comfortable.

bicycle pump

The first bikes didn't have tyres. Their wooden wheels
crunched along the road. They were very uncomfortable.
They were called **bone-shakers**.

Staying on the road

All vehicles need to stay on the road. Tyres help them to do this. They have a pattern on them called the **tread**. The tread helps the tyre to grip the road even when it's wet and slippery.

The tread makes the water run off the tyre. This helps the tyre to keep a grip on the road.

Tractor tyres have a very deep tread. That's because tractors work in fields where the ground is soft and slippery. Their wheels need a very good grip, otherwise they might get stuck in the mud.

Giant wheels help the tractor to move smoothly over the bumps.

Choosing tyres

Cyclists need the right kind of tyres for their bikes.

Cyclists who race along roads choose smooth, narrow tyres that are light and fast.

Cross-country cyclists need stronger, heavier tyres that can stand up to bumpy tracks.

Racing bikes are light and fast.

Mountain bikes are good for cycling cross-country.

Racing drivers change their tyres with the weather!
If the weather is dry, they use smooth tyres called **slicks**.
But if it rains, they choose tyres with a tread. The tread
stops them skidding on the wet track.

slicks

wet weather tyres

Wheels without tyres

Not every kind of vehicle has tyres.
A train has metal wheels which run along
smooth metal rails. The train glides along
easily and quickly.

The wheels don't slip off the track because
of their shape.

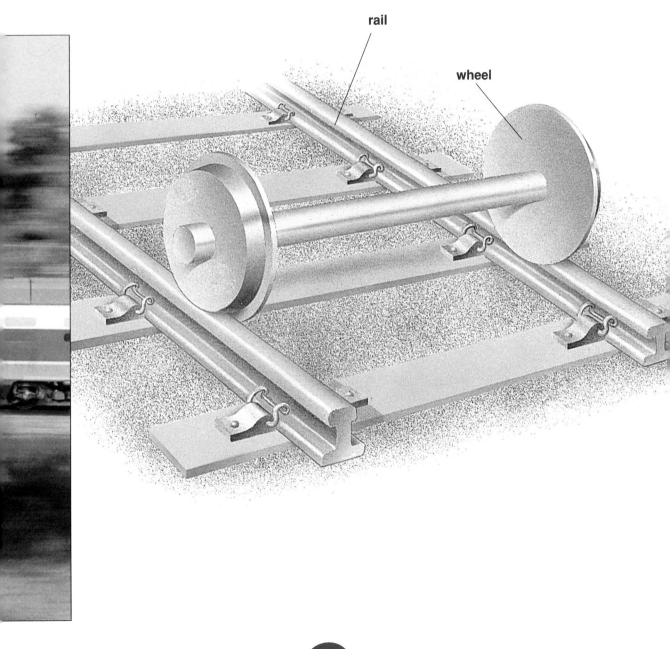

rail

wheel

Did you know?

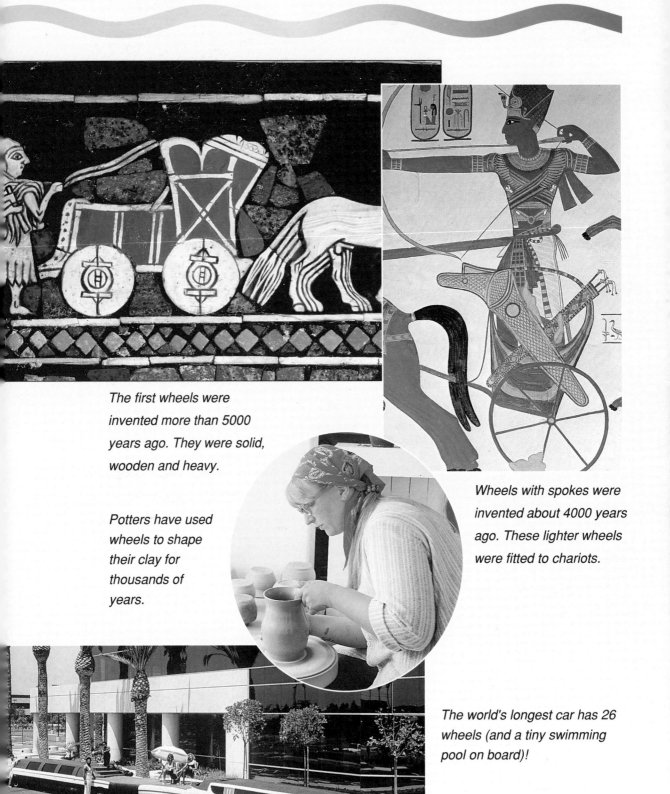

The first wheels were invented more than 5000 years ago. They were solid, wooden and heavy.

Potters have used wheels to shape their clay for thousands of years.

Wheels with spokes were invented about 4000 years ago. These lighter wheels were fitted to chariots.

The world's longest car has 26 wheels (and a tiny swimming pool on board)!

The biggest wheel you're likely to see is the huge Ferris wheel at the fair.

The biggest-ever bicycle wheel was made in the 1870s for the **penny-farthing**. It could go very fast!

Even some boats have wheels. Paddle-steamers' wheels have wide boards called **paddles**. As the wheels turn, the paddles push against the water, and move the boat along.

The biggest tyres in the world are made for hard-working dumper trucks. The tyres are about three times taller than a seven-year-old child!

Index